Being Beautifully Strong

Into your twenties and beyond

REBECCA DOROTHY VALASTRO

All rights reserved.
ISBN: 0-9954253-6-1
ISBN-13: 978-0-9954253-6-1
Published 2017.

All rights reserved. No part of this book may be reproduced by any mechanical, photographic, or electronic process, or in the form of a phonographic recording; nor may it be stored in a retrieval system, transmitted, or otherwise be copied for public or private use-other than for "fair use" as brief quotations embodied in articles and reviews-without prior written permission of the publisher.

The author of this book does not dispense medical advice or prescribe the use of any technique as a form of treatment for physical, emotional, or medical problems without the advice of a physician, either directly or indirectly. The intent of the author is only to offer information of a general nature to help you in your quest for emotional and spiritual well-being. In the event you use any of the information in this book for yourself, which is your constitutional right, the author and the publisher assume no responsibility for your actions.

BECAUSE WHY?

It's simple.
You are amazing,
You deserve the best and it's time you felt it
every single day.

After writing 365: Positive Words for a Teenage Girl, based on the "warm fuzzies" I received in my first year in highschool, other women told me, "I need a book like this."

So I drew upon a diary I began writing when I was sixteen years old, adding many affirmations as the years went by.

Every morning and night, I would read a page or two and sometimes ten or more. In the moments (days-weeks-months) that I did not read my diary of affirmations, I felt not quite as light, happy or confident. As soon as I returned to reading the pages, I felt stronger, happier, with the will to follow my dreams.

Reading these pages morning and night, begins and ends my day in a positive frame of mind, helping me to stay strong, determined, focused on the good in me and the good that is around me. In my eyes every woman is beautiful, just like every girl is and as we grow into our own uniqueness, it's our inner self-worth that gives us sustaining happiness. That's what keeps us strong, motivated and good to others. Being Beautifully Strong is the inner beauty and strength that gets us what we want.

It's so important to take care of ourselves first (and I'm not talking of ignoring the needs of others, like your children), but if we don't take care of ourselves, then how are we supposed to give to others, if we ourselves are empty? I am worth the time and effort to take care of me and all those around me benefit from it, for when I feel good and can honestly smile at the world... the world generally smiles back.

-from my heart to yours-
A piece of my inner strength.

B xxx

I AM

Beautiful

Intelligent

Thoughtful

Caring

Honest

I accept and welcome love and inner peace into my life. I am beautiful in every way and I give myself permission to focus on me. By filling me up first, I am able to give more to others. I now continue on my path, giving attention only to that which I want to create in my life and for my life; which is for the greater good of myself and those who are around me.

> There is no rulebook to say I cannot change my mind. I can change my mind at any moment and then I can change it again.

Today I give myself
permission
to make choices
that are right for me.

I see myself as
an extraordinary woman.
I am kind and beautiful.
I love what I see in me.

I shine on the inside as much as I shine on the outside. As I shine, I brighten up other people's day.

> Feeling is the key. When a thought feels good, it's doing me good. When a thought feels sad, whether it's someone else who did something to me or not, it only makes _me_ feel bad... not them. They don't feel what I feel.
>
> So today I choose to feel good. I choose a positive thought or phrase to replace the negative ones.
>
> Try and have a positive thought and make yourself feel bad at the same time —it's impossible. Make yourself feel good today, choose a positive thought instead.

Embrace where you are right now. Here (as in this moment) is a result of your past thoughts and actions. The greatest part about this moment right now, is that you are creating the new of everything in your life, from this moment forward. So don't sit in the past. Don't think of it, repeating it in your mind constantly -it's already done. Each moment is unfolding as the last one passes, so think amazing thoughts, see amazing things happening for you and each new moment will start to be more amazing and you will feel more amazing too.

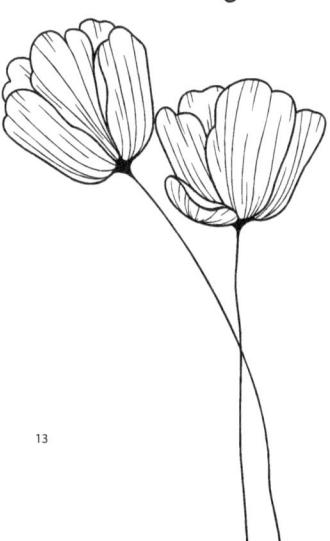

Being Beautifully STRONG

I Am Worthy of Great Love

YOU ARE AMAZING!

I truly mean that!

"

Let's be honest...

I am pretty AMAZING!

Did you laugh at that one?
I hope so... feels good to smile.

FYI... you are pretty amazing :-)

I SHINE BRIGHT

In every sense of the word.

Brightly
Emanating Beauty
Kind
Loving
Beautiful Nature

That is me.

A new life is a new beginning.

Being afraid to start over is totally normal. It's always hard when we first start out, like when we learnt to walk, took our first job, had our first heartbreak, became a mom.

If your heart is telling you to start a new job, find new friends, move house, leave a bad relationship...

do you think you should listen to it? Your happiness is worth breaking through the initial fear, because a new beginning brings the possibility of new opportunities.

To know peace, to feel love, to be in harmony… sometimes we have to experience the opposites; sadness, grief, anger, greed. Those feelings themselves aren't bad… but they are linked to experiences that feel bad. You can forgive yourself and move into the feelings you deserve —those of joy and happiness.

Being Beautifully STRONG

"

Every day I am my more perfect me.

Just by being myself, I make others happy.

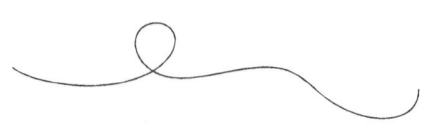

A wise man once told me, "Hurt people, hurt people." Sounds cryptic? I didn't get it at first, but then I realized what he meant... someone who is happy and whole inside, would never need to hurt another, lash out at another, say a mean thing to another. Someone who is deeply in pain, will cause pain to others and not necessarily consciously do it. When we are in pain and we are hurting, it's hard to see the good, the positive. We act defensively, we may even hurt others. I'm not making this behavior OK because it isn't, I just wanted you to know, that you can choose to let it go. You can choose to see that the person is in pain, that you are not the problem; a hurt person will hurt. You can choose to let them go, you can choose not to react, you can choose not to take on their shit. You are in control of you... and when you are hurting, remember these words, for no one is immune to the circle of causing and feeling pain. Be the person who deals with her hurt, deals with her shit, so that what you pass onto others is love and compassion.

Sometimes things don't go to plan - don't stress. Sometimes it's because something better is at work, whether it's as complex as having your wheels clamped on your car and having to wait an hour for them to be removed and while you wait, you meet the man of your dreams and a year later you're getting married (true story, happened to my friend). Or maybe it's more simplistic, like you have to go back home for your wallet cause you left it on the bench and in doing so, you missed the five-car pile-up on the freeway. Sometimes the things that happen in our life are not just coincidences. Sometimes a greater force is guiding us, protecting us, leading us to the path that we should be on. Perhaps that's an angel, God or just your very own instincts. Whatever it is, instead of feeling angry when these instances occur, take a deep breath and say thank you. You never know what miracle has just taken place... perhaps there was no miracle at all, but it sure does feel good to be grateful instead of angry.

I can say NO to others and YES to me first.

No is not a bad word.

I choose the best for me because I am worth it.

If I feel pressured in a conversation,
I can choose to respond with,
"Sounds great.
Let me get back to you."
I can then go away and make
choices that are right for me, without
being convinced of doing what
somebody else wants for me.

> I haven't always made the best decisions, but that doesn't mean I don't know how. I can listen to that inner voice, because deep down I know what is right for me. I am learning to trust myself with each day that passes.

> Time is on my side.
> I can take all the time I need
> to make the right choices for me.

I take time to reflect on important decisions.

If you can dream it,
It can happen.

If you can imagine it,
You can make it happen.

I create my life.
I am in charge of me.
I am in charge of my life.

What is it that I want to create in my life?

You Can Do It.

I remove judgment and I choose to see the benefit, the positive side. Even if it's not quite clear and the situation has created further challenges, I can choose to breathe and see the good… seeing just one positive, one lesson learnt, one something that could generate some good, not only makes me feel better but helps me to deal with what needs to happen next.

I promote, give, show and express unconditional love and positivity to everyone. I do not judge nor tell other people how to live their lives, nor try to change them or take away their choice to choose what is best for them. If it is hard for me to be around them, I can leave the friendship, relationship, acquaintanceship. It's everybody's right to live as the person they choose to be, just as it is my right to choose who is in (and not in) my life and the person I want to be.

Words are just words. It seems crazy
I know, but if someone calls me a
horrible name, it really shouldn't hurt
me at all. Why do I care so much? I know
that I am a good person. I am loving and
kind. If you call me a "bitch" – I choose
to feel like I am AMAZING instead of
feeling sad and angry, with a need
to change your mind. I know I don't ever
try to hurt anyone deliberately.
I am learning, I am growing. No matter
what age I am, I am always learning. So
today I choose to let go of the hurt behind
the words. I let others have their opinion
and I allow me to have my
own opinion of me.

It's my choice to move out of sadness and into gratitude and peace. Feel the feelings (yes even the bad ones), really allow yourself to feel them, and then move through it. Feel it and then let those feelings go. You can choose to live in those feelings miserably, or choose to observe them, like a fly sitting on the wall. The feelings are there and they may totally suck... but when you can observe them, you can choose to let them go. You can choose not to allow those feelings to hurt you anymore. Your past and the feelings attached to those experiences, are not who you are. You don't need your past to define who you are, where you are or where you are going. You can let the past go and free yourself from the pain you've associated with those experiences.

66

You can learn to be OK.

You deserve to be loved exactly as you are.

I can change.
I can release my past.
I can release the hurt.

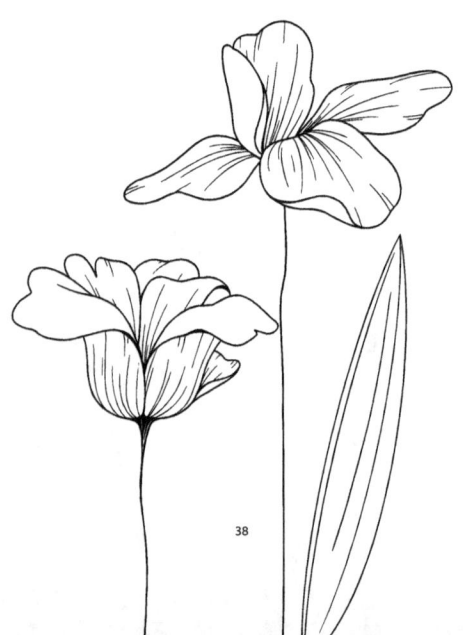

I LOVE & TRUST MYSELF

> By concentrating on me,
> I'm actually able to give more.
> When I am full, it's easy to splash
> out and give more of me to others.

I am a loving and
giving kind person.
I give to all, simply by being
my lovable self.

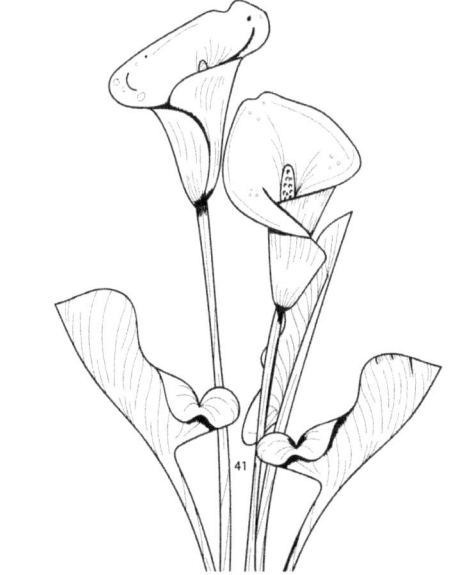

Do you think about a lot of things
that you don't want to happen?
Like - how am I ever going to buy a house?
Or - I always feel fat or ugly?
And - I never get the job/guy/car I want?

Notice what you are thinking. Do you love
those thoughts that you just gave your
attention to? I'm guessing they make you
feel bad about yourself.

It's time to put your attention on the things
you would love to happen. Change your
thoughts by focusing on the things you
really want in your life. What you pay
attention to grows, so grow the things you
truly want and give none of your energy
to that which you do not want.

Every time a negative thought pops into my head, I choose a positive thought instead. It's easy to do. I just choose a different phrase that makes me feel good.

Try imagining the opposite to the negative thought; something you want to happen instead, like - I have the perfect body for me, it feels so good to save for the house/car I want and attract a great guy for me.

Are you smiling now?

Good thoughts = Good feelings
You deserve to feel good every single day.

The more you focus on it, good or bad, your attention is creating it.

Focus on all the good currently in your life and then on the things you really want in your life. When you focus on what you want, you begin to do what's necessary to make those things happen. When focusing on the absence of something, it demotivates you and stops you from taking the steps to get you where you want to be.

What are you focusing on today?
Make sure it's something you actually want.

What would you do if you knew you couldn't fail, that success was guaranteed?

OK – now do it!

I can choose to see at
least one positive
in every person.

I AM KIND

Enjoy every minute you have with each person... you never know when it is your last moment together.
There is one life for all of us.
Live it, Love it, Be Present in it.

Live each day with so much love,
as though it was your last day.

Knowing that I have today,
fills me with energy.

Find the message in the fear you are feeling. Begin by acknowledging that the fear is there, then write down the specifics of what you are fearing. Can you turn that fear into humor, like the giant scary spider in Harry Potter that was given roller skates and couldn't stand up. Yeah it's real silly I know, but sometimes exaggerating the fear can help us to reduce the fear. For instance the fear of being lonely -if I make it as ridiculous as me living on an island with no books, no internet, no people, no music, no animals, no sun, no waves, no trees blowing in the wind; just absolutely nothing... well, by doing that, I can see that I am never truly alone. Helps me to appreciate what I do have around me.

If you are experiencing life crippling fears, or fears that make you want to harm yourself or others, then please speak with a medical professional immediately. Your safety and happiness, as well as those around you, is the highest priority.

When we stop long enough to hear the silence, we can then listen to find the reason why we are in a particular situation.

Quiet your mind long enough to find the reasons why. Really listen to that inner knowing. Knowing the reason means you know the answer too.

When you feel fear, shift your attention to your highest purpose. Imagine yourself at your very best, surrounded by love & friendship.

I can find the answers.
I can find a solution.
I have faith in my ability
to take care of me.

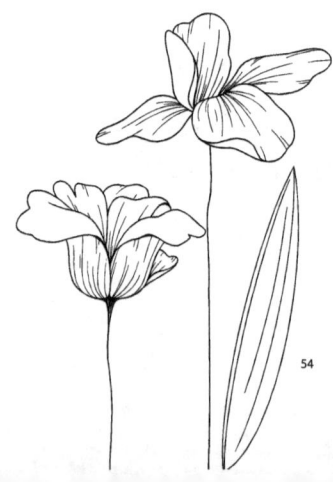

Every day is a brand new day,
You get to reinvent yourself.

Who do you choose to be today?

Everything I want, I get.
Everything I say, I do.

I have great power within me.

I Truly Am BEAUTIFUL

In Fact I Am STUNNING!

I will not compromise my dreams.

I am worth living all the possibilities I have dreamed up for me. Someone who loves me, would never ask me to compromise my soul -that is where dreams come from. Love doesn't stifle or drain, nor does it ask me to give up that part of me that makes me feel whole. Our dreams are important. We live one life... just the one.

It's meant to be lived in joy.

"

The path that I have set for me, is leading me to my destiny. I do not allow fear to slow me down, whether it is fear of failure or fear of age. The only limitations that I face, are the ones I place on myself.

Today I choose to have no limitations on me.

Today I Live Fearlessly

I am loyal and brave,
strong and open.
I am here, loving to all.
And I AM Happy.

> Great things are coming to me everyday AND I feel great!

I Can Stand Strong.
And I do.

*Every Day in Every Way
My Life gets Better & Better.*

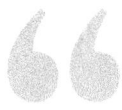

It is OK to ask for help.
It is smart to do so.

> I ask for support.
> It's there when I need it.

I surround myself with people
who love and care for me.

I surround myself with people
who treat me with kindness.

It is safe for me to look within. I am a good person. I can forgive my past, I can forgive myself. I did the best I could with the knowledge that I had.

> It is safe for me to love. It isn't love that breaks hearts, it's love that mends them. I can choose to love all people.

As I live each day,
I trust that I will know
what next to do,
where I am meant to go.
I will hold the idea of where it is
that I want to be and I trust
that the next step to take
will be revealed to me.

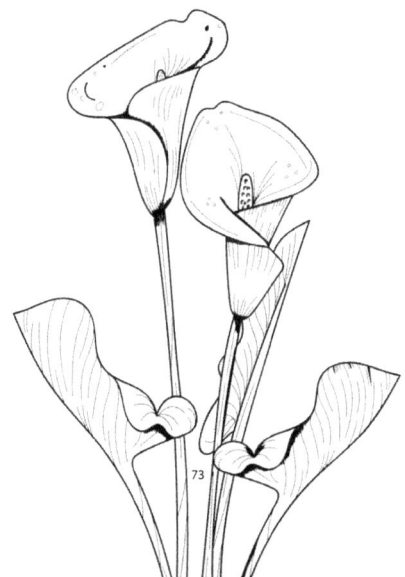

I trust in the choices
that I make for myself today.
Even if some of my past decisions
haven't turned out exactly how
I hoped, those past decisions
made me better at the choices
I make today.

I Trust Me.

Being Beautifully STRONG

"

I am a Strong
Confident Woman

I emanate care, kindness
and understanding.

Every day I am getting stronger & stronger.

Today I let go of other people's opinions and beliefs about me. I have a beautiful soul. I love being me.

People will always remember how you make them feel... Choose your words wisely; you are kind, smart and have so much compassion within you.

I am truthful and honest
I am loving and giving
I am positive & kind
I am wonderful
I am amazing
I am full of potential
I am absolutely intelligent

I am ME!

I am proud of all that I have achieved.
I am proud of all that I am achieving.
I am proud of my determination.
I am proud of my perseverance.
I am proud of how much I love.
I am proud of how much I care.
I am proud of my amazing self.

I am proud of ME.

I ask for what I want and
I know that it is mine.

See the outcome, before it happens. Feel how good it is to have what you want and live as though it already is.

Today I take a chance on me
-on something I truly desire.

Perseverance
Perseverance
Perseverance

I Never Give Up!

> I Love life!
> I Love My Life!
> Life Loves Me!
> Life Supports Me!

Stay focused. Get it done.
Give it everything you've got,
every second, every day.

-it's worth it!

Stop thinking about it.
Put your Plan into Action.

I Am Focused
I Take Action Now.

I live with passion and purpose.

No purpose is small or meaningless. Purpose is what you live for. Purpose uplifts others. Like a mother whose purpose is to love and grow those special little human beings, or for the sales assistant to bring excellent customer service that puts joy into other people's day, or the nurse that eases the pain of a patient and the writer who writes in hope to inspire. Every single purpose is worth the passion you put into it.

Create your own Stars

If you can dream it,
you can make it happen!

Map it out, write it down, Plan, take action and most importantly believe. Don't give up. It takes time, but our dreams are worth it.

When you visualize finishing your goal, you actually pave a way of how to finish the goal. If you can see yourself achieve it, then you certainly can find a way to get it done.

I Am Capable!

I am Extraordinary

I have a very important job to do, being me.

Put the image of your
ultimate life in your mind.
Feel how good it feels to live this life.
Now carry that wonderful feeling
with you all day. And every time
something happens that brings you
out of that happy feeling, imagine
that ultimate life and start feeling
the good feelings again.
Feeling good can be a choice.

You can ask yourself,
why am I here in this situation?
What needs to happen in order
for me to move forward?
If you are blissfully happy,
then you can be grateful
for all that is...

And if you're searching for more,
you can find the answers within.

Write on a piece of paper or simply just think about all the things you have achieved. From shooting that goal in basketball as a kid, right up to getting your first job, going on that holiday and being blessed enough to have fallen in love. See all the work you have put into your life and feel inspired again. Your life is truly unique; as are you... and the person you should be most proud of, is you.

"

Clarify what you are doing.

It's easier to get where I want to go when I clarify what it is that I want and what I am going to do to get me there. When you see the steps, you can take the steps. It's the many steps we take that get us to the top.

I believe in me.
I believe in what I am doing.

I Am Full of Confidence & I Feel Great.

I accept and love myself exactly how I am right now.

I am a good, loving, caring person.

"

I have the freedom to be myself, my true self, here and now and nothing can stand in my way.

It is safe for me to trust myself and I know I can trust my instincts. I listen to that feeling inside and act accordingly.

Fear of not being able to do something you love, is a waste of your precious heart.

Today I choose to believe in me.

I fill my body with goodness.

I have a perfect body!

"

I have a perfect nose, face and body.

I am stunning,
I am amazing,
I am beautiful.

I just so happen to be photogenic too!

I don't have to feel shy. I can smile knowing, my smile makes you smile too.

Whether people think this book
is wish-washy or silly to do
affirmations ... I want you
to know, you really
do deserve the best.

Choose who you listen to, what you read and what you watch carefully. Do what feels right to you.

Even if that's putting this book in the bin.

If it doesn't feel good, don't do it.

Today I choose to feel good, because I am worth it!

Today I'm just gonna smile at everyone, because when I smile at the world, it generally smiles back. Even the people who are sad, lonely, having a bad day...
they may not smile back at me externally, but there is a tiny smile in their heart that makes them feel a little bit better inside.

You never know whose day you might change from simply giving them a smile. WE ALL have had days where we wanted to give up, we wanted to hide away, even days where we may not have wanted to wake up. When someone smiles at you or says a kind word, it can be the one thing that gets you to the next step. It can be the one thing that makes you choose to live.
Who can you smile at today?

What do you most value?

Can you set aside time today
honoring what they are?

If it's friendship
—take your bestie to the movies

If it's your children
—paint a picture with them

If it's love
—express it in a special way

If it's your sanity
—do something special for you

What are the 3 most important things in your life?

Can you rearrange your time so that these take priority today?

> I no longer tire.
>   I am Full of Life.
>   I Feel Energized.

I Am Strong, I Am Independent & I Am Free.

I Feel Happiness Everyday.

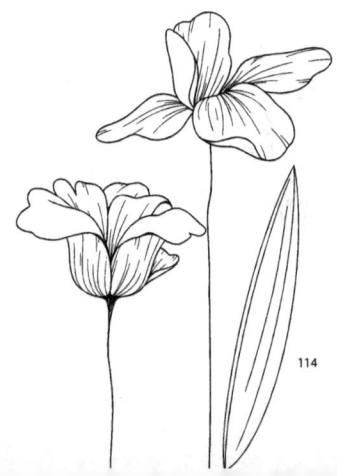

Life gives me all
that I want and
all that I need.

66

I accept & welcome
happiness & love
into my life.

I put aside all that limits me.

I am limitless.
I am free.
I am me.

I am beautiful
I am kind
I am intelligent
I am friendly
I am strong

I am Proud of me.

You've done an amazing job, being you.

"

I take good care
of ME today.

"

Don't let anyone suck you into an argument.
You choose anger. You are in control. Nasty words aren't worth the damage they do, nor the energy you waste. Your time is more valuable than that ... and so are you.

I choose the windows of
opportunity that are open to me.
I move on from my past and
I no longer tap on the doors that
are closed. I see the beauty in
a new day, which is full of
new possibilities for me.

I am connected to my emotions.
I can express myself clearly and calmly.

I consider all options, information and the situation. I trust in the choices I make.

Take a look around at your environment. Are you storing papers, boxes, piles of clothes? Can you take action today and clear away the clutter? Release what you are holding onto.

The physical environment around us can indicate what is going on inside of us. Get clear on your life - get clear in your head. Clear the clutter and free your mind.

What do I want?
I'm allowed to ask for it.
I'm allowed to have it.
It is OK to put me first.
My wishes, hopes & dreams,
should be respected not only by me,
but also by those who are around me.

Connect with something beautiful. Really see a tree. Admire a flower. Look at yourself in the mirror or at someone else's smile. Stop for a moment to see the beauty and watch how it makes you feel inside. Let it warm you. Let it brighten your day. There is beauty everywhere (and yes annoyingly) in the most simplest of things. When we shift our negative thoughts to something beautiful instead, we feel good. For some reason it starts to make us smile. Everybody's image of beauty is different. Can the sun make you smile? The beauty of autumn leaves, or a really well made ice-cream sundae (that's my go to comfort food). Whatever it is, feel it. Close your eyes and feel how good it feels to feel the joy in something that is beautiful to you.

Breathe.

When you feel yourself starting to panic, take 3 really slow long breaths in and out.

If it helps, count in for 6 and out for 6.

repeat:

I am Calm & Centered

When fighting, arguing, disagreeing with another, you can ask yourself, what is it I want exactly? Why do I need to win here? Does it really matter if I don't win?
If I'm not listening to them and they aren't listening to me, then all I hear is my own harsh words. When you are too busy working out what next to yell, to convince each other why you are both right -your words end up doing more harm to you, then they do to them.

Repeating profanities in your head is like swearing directly at yourself
(even though you meant it at them).

When I feel anxious, hurt or angry,

I can choose to stop and ask myself,

why do I need to feel this way?

Do I need to hold onto this feeling?

or can I let it go away?

It doesn't hurt the other person while

I hold onto it -It only hurts me.

Today I choose to Let it Go, so that

I feel lighter, more balanced and at peace.

I am calm

"

I am focused on here & now
in this moment.

I am in charge of my choices and
limitations. No one limits me and
I choose to have no limitations
in my life nor on me.
I choose who I am and I choose
to move forward.

I release all my limitations.
There is no limit to what
I can achieve.

I let go of need. How can I expect anything outside of myself to fulfill me, when I am the one who is in full control of me and every emotion that I feel. Yes it is hard at times to choose joy over hurt, anger or pain, but there is nothing truly outside of myself that can make everything right inside of me, except for me. Today I choose to give myself a break. I allow myself to feel joy, to feel happy.

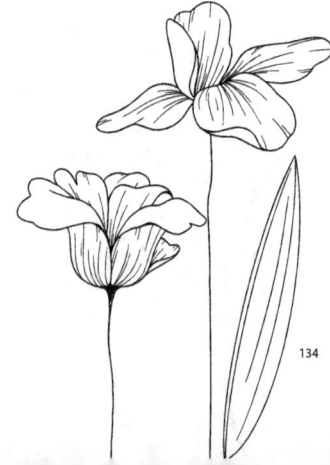

I am completely responsible for my life.
I make the choices.
I make my rules.

> I let go of what does not bring me joy.
> If it is harmful, I don't need it,
> I can choose to let it go.

I have complete faith in myself and my ability to make the right decisions for me and for my life.

I believe in me and
I trust that I say and do the
right thing in each moment.

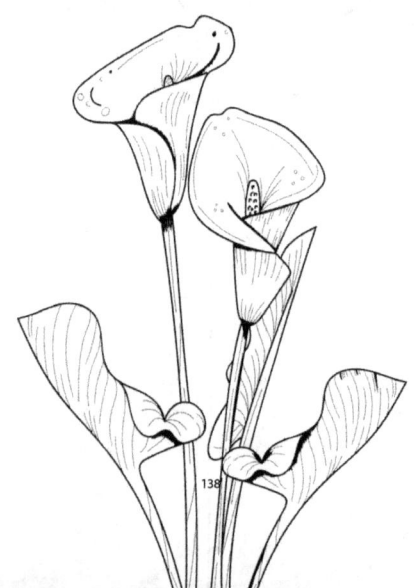

You do not have to stay in a relationship if it is destroying your soul. If you feel sad more than you feel good, then something is wrong. You decide what's best for you because you are worth every desire that you can imagine for yourself.

Don't look for the perfect mate, perfect yourself instead. Treat others how you want to be treated while focusing on achieving your goals. The perfect person will walk into your life, when you are living your life for you.

All choices are mine to make.
I need not fear making one,
for if it doesn't work out,
I can make another.

Mistakes are just learning curves.

I can forgive me

... and I do.

Staying focused on here and now allows me to be in this moment.

It's good to have goals and visualize them, as they also bring me joy. What I remind myself of today, is to feel joy in the process of living, for today shall pass, as do all days and this precious moment will fade.

I can live with both the joy of the future, of where I am going, while enjoying this moment today.

It's not right for me to make others wrong, when we have walked in completely different shoes. No two lives are exactly the same. We all experience life differently.

I know wrong from right,
but I don't make others wrong
because I think that I am right.

Why am I angry with you?

Why do I need you to change?

Do I have an unfair expectation of you?

All valid questions only YOU can answer. If you feel unhappy more than you feel happy when you are around a particular person, it is OK to let them go. If we cannot accept people the way they are, if all we want to do is change them, then it is best we let them go. You can never truly change another person. They have to make that choice for themselves.

Today I let others decide who they want to be, just as I choose who I want to be.

> People only factor in what they know, what they have read, what they have experienced. Don't take anybody's word as gospel. People repeat what they heard from a friend, what they read on the Internet or saw on the news.
>
> These are just people's opinions. Don't feel as though you know nothing in comparison, or that you have to believe what they tell you. Always investigate for yourself, because people will always give you advice whether they are an expert or not and whether you asked for it or not.
>
> There is a lot of mumbo jumbo out there -don't take anything as truth, not even this book! If it doesn't feel good, if it doesn't fit into your values, then don't do it, don't read it and make the choice for yourself and not because someone else told you, you should or shouldn't believe it.

Never feel offended. People don't know you, the way you know you, so who cares what they think about you. Nobody ever really has the full story. Unless they have lived your life, they don't really know your life.

Today I relax knowing, I am a good person.

Holding onto anger and onto the past, only hurts you. No one else knows what you are thinking about, nor how badly it affected you. The person you hurt by constantly thinking about it, is you.

Today I forgive because it's the best thing I can do for myself.

I choose my destiny

-pick a good one that makes you happy-

I am provided with everything I need.

I deserve to have every happiness in the world, in my life right now.

Yes you really do!

I see my worth.
I am special.
I am compelling magnificent!

I radiate beauty, health, love and kindness. I shine like the brightest star!

I count. I truly matter.
I truly make a difference
in other people's lives.

> The world is a beautiful place
> & I am a beautiful girl.

I deserve the very best in Life.
I deserve to be Loved.

I now ask for what I want
and I can relax knowing, that by
working toward it, I can
have what I want.

I appreciate the uniqueness in
all the beauty that surrounds me.
I see beauty and uniqueness in me.

> You don't have to stay anywhere that makes you feel unhappy. You are here to be loved, to celebrate and live life. If you find that you are sad and feel trapped, lean on people around you. If you are in an unsafe environment, please reach out and get professional support and help. There are so many of us across the globe that are here for each other, that want the best for one another. Never feel alone because you are not and if you feel afraid please let someone know, for no one should live in constant pain nor constant fear.
>
> It is OK for me to reach out for support. If I cannot trust anyone close to me, then I can choose to call a helpline or even the police.

You can't really blame anyone else for the situation you are in - the job you hate, the marriage, the social event, even the abusive relationship. At some point you knew it was wrong. Whether we like to admit it or not, we ignore the instinct, that feeling inside telling us not to do it, take it, love it.

It's going to be OK. It takes years, sometimes a whole lifetime to listen to that inner voice... and not just listen to it (cause often we do hear it), but to trust it. To act on it. Knowing that you can make better choices for you, is the first step for change. It can be scary going into a new job or new relationship or even making another decision after we've made choices that have hurt us, but acknowledging it, is the first step to trusting yourself again. It's the first step in seeing that you deserve more, that you are worth more. I truly believe it is your birthright to feel great - to be loved. You deserve it and you should have it.

Leaving a friendship, family member or partner, especially with kids, is difficult, scary and heartbreaking. Chances are, you already know the right thing to do. You feel it in your heart.

Place your hand over your heart and shut your eyes. This may seem silly, but simply ask your heart what it wants and what to do. It knows. It won't deceive you.

I Trust my Heart

Sometimes all you need to do to move forward is decide. Make a choice.

We are often feeling stuck because we are too afraid to make one choice or another. Not making a choice IS making a choice. It's choosing to stay stuck in that moment.

I make clear decisions.
I make the right choices for me.

> I Live Passionately
>
> I'm not afraid to be who I am.

I Am Open

I'm willing to trust people & life

Have you seen the movie Pollyanna?

I feel like this was the message from that movie: if you are constantly negative, you put yourself in misery and you push out all the good in your life. When you start to focus on one small positive thing, you begin to feel good and it has a knock-on effect on those who surround you. Of course it is your right to be sad when you are going through a tough time, but ask yourself - how long has this tough time been weighing me down? Isn't it time you felt good?

I know sometimes affirmations can feel stupid and not real... but it's a start. As you begin to feel more joy, pick 5 things you are thankful for and every morning really feel how grateful you are for those 5 things. You'll be amazed at how much better you can feel by simply shifting your attention to something that generates good feelings. I apologize for saying "simple" - I know it's not. But the more you do it, the more simple it becomes and the more you feel good.

Please speak to a medical professional if you feel down all the time. They can help you.

I Feel at Peace with
Myself & Others.

> I am here for others and myself.
> I care about <u>All</u> of us.

Thank you for the abundance of love and success I have in my life.

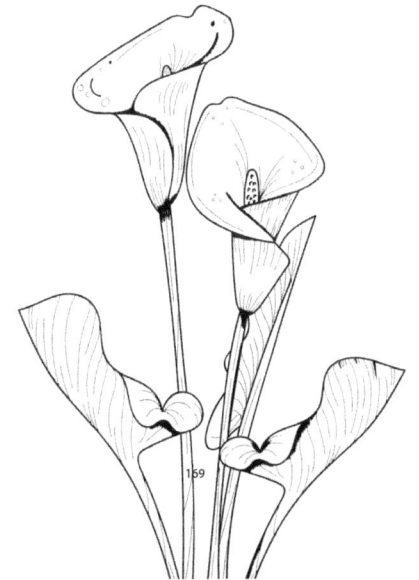

Nothing is Impossible
Only mathematically improbable.

I love this saying! I have no idea who said it, nor where it came from -it certainly isn't mine.

I was 15 years old when I started repeating this saying. I truly believed it. Life has been hard. It has really sucked at times. But I know true in my heart, that I can be, do and have, all that I want in this world. I just have to believe and do the work to achieve.

I truly am Limitless...
and it's time I truly Believed it!

"

I am Vibrant & Healthy

I Shine Bright

Being Beautifully STRONG

List the great qualities that you can see in yourself.

Write them down on a piece of paper and read them every day, especially when you are feeling low. Remind yourself of how wonderful you are.

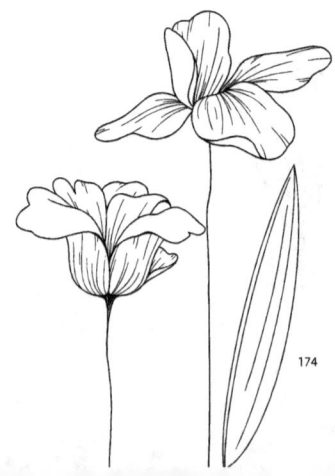

Now list the great qualities that other people see in you.

It's good to remind yourself of all the wonderful things that other people can see in you.

A promise to myself...

To live in joy!
To always believe in me!
To allow the world to see me for who I really am... a kind, loving person that is here to have fun, to love, to be free -to be ME.

I am a great person…
and by living my purpose,
by living what makes me happy,
I bring joy to other people's lives.

You know you can be whoever you want to be. Reinvent yourself today. Be whatever, whoever, however you want to be.

One Life – Be Bold

External events cannot destroy your dreams unless you allow them to. Let go of the illusion that you cannot change your life today.

Today I make the necessary changes that make me happy. Today I choose to live in Joy.

> Think about 3 really great things in your life and say thank you. Really feel how good those things make you feel. It can be as simple as a really good cup of coffee or as important as your legs that allow you to walk or even the petrol in your car -AND the car itself that takes you where you need to go. Good friends is another one. I'm really grateful for the supportive people in my life.

Stay clear headed

Don't force it
Don't obsess
Let it go

That which is right for you, doesn't need to be forced. You are worth the best in life. Don't waste your time on those that don't see it or nurture it. You're just too special and too amazing to not feel joy in every moment.

Today I make good choices for me. I surround myself with people who are kind like me.

I deserve & attract all the wonderful qualities in a partner that I also have in me.

"

Do you feel threatened, guilty, stuck or frozen in a conversation? You might be wrapped up in a power struggle.

Stop and take three slow breaths in and out. Repeat to yourself; I am strong, I am loving, I am understanding. I trust myself to know when to speak, when to listen and when to walk away.

If someone in your life is
constantly putting you down,
you can simply say to them,
"When I am with you,
I feel put down. Is there something
else bothering you?"

People tend to pick, not because they
don't like you, but because they
don't like themselves. You may save
a friendship and help someone else
at the same time, by simply
asking if they are OK.

When you are talking to someone and you feel like they aren't really listening to you, it's OK to choose to say to them, "I feel like you are somewhere else. Are you OK?"

It's best to ask and not presume. They may have something on their mind, that you can help with. Instead of feeling like it's you who is the problem; just ask. The problem most likely isn't you.

If you find yourself arguing with someone, trying to convince them and defending your beliefs. Is the defensiveness needed? Or does it get in the way of hearing what is being said?

Today I remain open.

With people who intimidate me, I can simply ask them calmly, "Why are you so angry? Do you want me to be afraid of you?"

Sometimes we don't realize how we affect other people and it is OK to say, it's not OK.

I see truth & real emotions.

I see beyond the drama to the <u>Real</u> person inside.

I can be understanding.
I can choose to listen.

I let go of angry people in my life. I deserve to be treated with respect, just as I treat others with respect.

I am beautiful and unique.
I deserve to be loved by everyone,
just as I can find within myself,
love for others.

"

I take the time to listen to others.
Most people have good hearts.
It's up to me to see it.

Today I choose to see how wonderful I truly am and that I am worth every joy in life.

I am only responsible for myself. I do not blame or judge based on where I am at, nor do I compare myself to others. We are all different, achieving different things at different times. That's what makes us all special. We can inspire each other.

It's in your past with others, that you can find forgiveness. It's in your past together, because of the moments you shared together, that you can forgive. Think of a really happy moment, a long time ago, a special moment, a moment of love or laughter. It is from there that you can forgive.

I deserve to be loved with absolute passion and commitment. I deserve to be treated with respect and asked if I am OK. What I deserve is exactly what I put forward. I deserve all the wonderful things that I can see for me.

When you stay in an abusive relationship, whether it's a friend, family member or partner, you are showing yourself how little you are worth. The thing is, you are worth THE WORLD. You are amazing and wonderful, beautiful and strong. You are kind and caring and giving too. You deserve the most precious love with laughter and fun. You are worth so much more.

VIOLENCE IS NOT OK

It is not OK for anyone to hit, push or touch you. No one has the right to do so. If someone is hurting you, you have the right to say no and you have the right to tell someone about it, to ensure it does not happen again. Your body is sacred and special and it is yours and only yours. Say no to those who would act in violence against you and if you notice violence against someone else, tell someone so it can stop. Violence is not OK. Say NO to violence.

It is my birthright to be spoken to with love, care and respect. It is OK for me to walk away from those who would harm me. It is OK for me to seek further help from authorities and professionals.

No problem is too small. There is support for me. All I need to do is call out and ask for help.

I no longer allow others to hurt me! I know the difference between abuse and a disagreement. I say NO to abuse.

If you feel sad more than you feel happy and this book isn't making a difference, then please seek professional help.
It is OK to do so.
Please take care of you.

That which is meant to be,
will be... at the right time.

It's time to trust in my ability to create a wonderful life for me.

It's my choices that define my life and today I choose to give myself the best life ever.

I can let go of the anxiety. That sick twisted worrying feeling inside never helps. Today I choose to develop an action plan and think kind thoughts about myself.

I trust in my vision for the future, so I let today take me where I need to go.
I trust and let go.

Choose something that makes you feel great as your vision for the future.

I believe in my success.
I believe in my dreams.
I believe in me.

I am succeeding & living more of my dreams each day.

If you find yourself playing out scenarios in your head and they are making you feel really bad -try and end the scenario with an outcome that would make you happy instead. Think of the most positive, best outcome that you can imagine and then let that thought go.

Life can be really difficult when we are worried about what is happening in our lives OR more so, what MAY happen. Keep repeating this process -end the thought or image in your head with a positive outcome instead.

If you can possibly let it go, then that will help you to live in this moment with a little less stress in your head.

If a negative thought or image comes into your mind, HALT IT and replace it with a good positive thought or image instead.

Try and do this all day and see if you can replace every negative thought with a positive one.

*little experiment
– did you end up having a good day?

Not only do I have the ability to learn new things and be a new person, I have the intelligence and willpower to perform any action that I desire. I can be whoever I want to be. I can do any job I choose to work toward. I am more capable than anyone else can see or imagine. And most importantly... I trust in me. I will take me where I want to go.

I forgive.

Who can you forgive today?
You no longer need the hurt
that's making you feel bad.

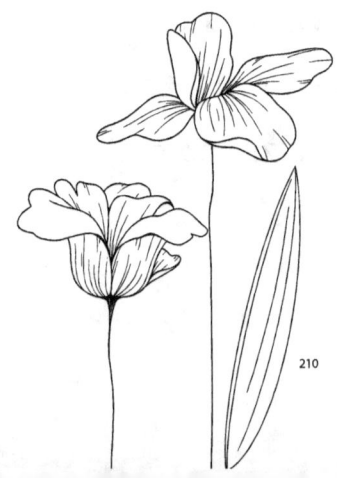

I LIKE ME ☺

I am beautiful.
I am full of love & compassion.
My mind is open and I am more
accepting of others as each day goes by.

This is what I call the

NO ANT PMA LG DDY KS HF HF

NO Automatic Negative Thoughts
Positive Mental Attitude
Let Go
Don't Doubt Yourself
Keep Smiling
Have Faith
Have Fun!

Repeat it all day long

I Feel Peaceful

On the days that I feel crazy, I sit and breathe. Calm slow breaths help me to focus.

I am a wonderful, loving, giving person.

Whatever happens, I can handle it. I have incredible strength within me.

Create your own fashion.

Let's be real... when you're dead, you won't give a crap, so wear what you want, when you want, how you want. You look fabulous always -it's just a matter of perspective... and trust me, only your perspective matters. So feel fabulous today in anything you wear.

"

I am energetic, fun, confident and talkative. People feel good when they are around me and when they walk away from me. I am nice and loving to all people. I leave people feeling better then when they arrived.

I show and give positivity
on a humongous massive
scale to All people.
I am here and giving to all.
I see the good in me.
I see the good in others.

I let conversation flow.

You never know what you might learn by really listening to others.

Asking questions is the best thing in life. It will get you out of an awkward conversation or an uncomfortable job interview, it'll make you better at your job and you will know more about other people then you could ever have imagined. Never be afraid to ask. No question is stupid, regardless of what anyone might say. Sometimes people brush you off because they don't know how to answer you or because they don't know the answer. Keep asking questions. Being curious is a good thing.

Today I am fearless in the questions I ask.

Your mood rubs off on others. How you feel translates into how you act and the way you act can impact the people around you. When you are happy and full of life, that rubs off on others too.

You can actually help being grumpy. Probably makes you mad to know that your mood is really controlled by you (sorry to break the bad news). Try not to get angry about it. Perhaps shift your thinking to something you love -a fond memory, a goal you wish to achieve. Think about something joyful. Don't get angry about it, move on, let go. Constantly complaining about other people won't help the situation. It's already happened. You can't change it, but you can change how you feel right now.

It's OK to be upset and grumpy, but if you ever get sick of it and want to feel good, you can use the little tool of thinking about something you love instead.

Blaming others
Being a victim
Becoming the chatterbox

Ask yourself, what are the payoffs
if I do the above?

Blaming others gives away your
power to take charge of your life.
You are a strong woman and
in control of your own life.

Being a victim by constantly telling the "poor me" story will keep you sad, even though you are a beautiful vivacious incredible woman, destined for greatness.

Becoming the chatterbox, where you are too busy talking about other people instead of connecting with those who are around you, by answering questions about your true self and your outlook on life, which people don't ask because they don't get a chance to ask, if you are too busy talking about others...

You're too good for that.

If you find yourself complaining or criticizing

HALT IT

Simply replace it with something positive. Whether it's a nice trait about the person you are complaining about or as simple as, 'it's a nice day.' You can find something... ☺

Other people can yell and scream...
I can simply walk away.
I continue to breathe.
If other people aren't willing
to talk to me calmly with respect,
then I can choose to walk away.

Fight or Flight we use in dangerous, life threatening situations. When your heart is pumping in an argument but your life isn't in danger -breathe. Walk away if you need to and keep breathing.

When words are yelled at us, we switch off and go into defense mode. We aren't listening. All you get from that situation is blame and anger.

Walk away and breathe. No one is winning anyway. Just because you say the most hurtful thing, bring up the past or lash out, doesn't mean you won.
No one wins.

Breathe. Walk away and Breathe.

Why be angry when you can be happy?
You choose your feelings.

I know some anger just came out of you. How can it not when you feel like, "It's not my fault such and such did this to me!"

I get it, I really really do. I have been exactly like you. But there is one thing I do know... if you can find one positive thing, just one thing you learned, one thing you gained or something huge like the children you got out of that past relationship, then that is the one positive you can focus on. The one thing you can be grateful for. Perhaps you didn't have children and now you're all alone... but he is still out there "the one" -isn't that awesome! You finally got out of something that made you so very sad and have the chance to be with someone so very right for you. I know it's not the same if you break a leg or lose a job... but is there one thing you can find? One something that you can be grateful for?

You'll be amazed at how much better you can feel by simply shifting your attention to something that generates good feelings.

I apologize for saying "simple" -I know it's not. But the more you do it, the more simple it is and the more it feels good too.

*Please speak to a medical professional if you feel down all the time. They can help you.

Can you find one positive in every situation?

Does it make you feel a little better? Feeling that one positive? If you feel no relief from the pain you are in, please seek professional advice. There are doctors, psychologist and helplines that are there to help you.

Every day when I look in the
mirror, I see a more amazing me.

Today I Feel Gratitude...
because simply being alive
is truly a great thing.

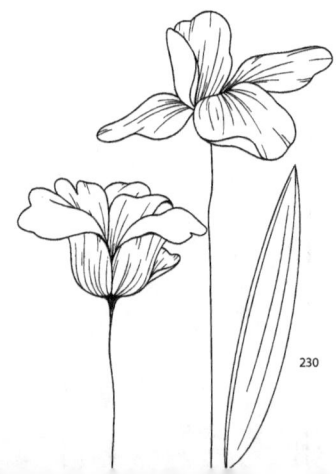

It's how we view the world, which makes us happy or not. Try having a positive thought and then another, then another. Positive thoughts feed you positivity, giving you positive energy and more positive thoughts.

Positive thoughts = feeling great.

The more you focus on it, good or bad, your attention is creating it.

What are you focusing on today? Make sure it's something that you actually want.

Me & My Feelings Are Important.

I will know which way to go. I trust me.

I am understanding of others.
I can be compassionate and
stand strong at the same time.

"

I respect myself.
My wishes and needs are important;
I respect those too.

Every day I grow more confident in my abilities and the person I choose to be.

I am clear minded, focused, energized, motivated and full of energy.

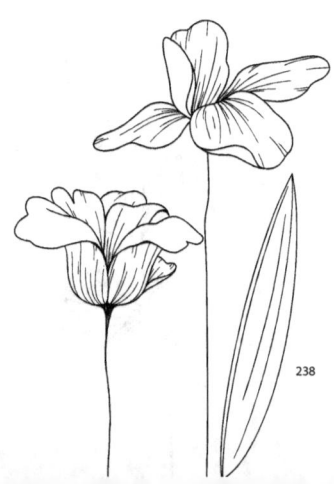

I am healthy, fit, and happy.
Life moves forward for me and I am excited!

> Today I am Full of Energy.
>
> Today I am Full of Life!

Releasing Fear

Clear your mind & close your eyes.

Focus on your breath
-slowly in & out.

Ask for guidance
-from your heart, God or an angel.

Focus on what you want to happen.
See the desired outcome.

Breathe the fear out.

How do you know where you are going, if you can't see where you are going?

See your success.
Visualize it.
Feel it.

Before you go to sleep at night visualize all the good in your life and all the good that is coming into your life.

By knowing where I am, I can plan for where I want to go. By knowing what I don't like, tells me what I do want for me. Knowing, acknowledging, then refocusing, begins the process of setting up the life I want for me.

"

All the choices I made
were right for me at the time.

There is no need for me to fear making a new choice
nor guilty. I will know what to do at the time.

The only person that limits me is me and I choose to have no limitations on me!

Everything is Possible ☺

At any time I can make a choice to change my life. Change is good. I welcome change with open arms.

I commit to living
My Goals, My Dreams.

I am committed to taking Care of Me.

66

I am capable!

I achieve everything I choose to!

There is no need for me to
feel guilty because of others.
We are all choosing our own lives.
I am allowed to be happy with
myself and with my life.

I am willing to change
and expand. It is OK to listen to
new people, read new books,
then decide what is right for me.
I give myself full support.

I focus on the unique beauty of each person I encounter. I choose to look within at who they really are.

I do not blame others for the situation
I am in. I am responsible for me.
I can change it. I can seek help.
It is up to me.

I choose to not focus on other people's traits that are irritating to me. It's not up to me to change them. I can accept them as they are or I can choose to walk away. Focusing on the negative drains myself and others.
We all deserve to feel full of life.

There are no wrong ways.
It's the choices you make and
if you don't like the direction
you are going in...
then make another choice.

I have faith in you.

Try having some faith
in you too.

We all deserve to be loved and treated with kindness.

Today I choose to express gratitude toward others.

I am completely one hundred percent loveable. I allow love into my life and I am open to beautiful and fun relationships.

I am both assertive and receptive. I can communicate without blame. I don't need to win an argument, as the only point I need to prove, is to myself. I can move forward.
I can release anger and drama out of my life.

I listen
I cooperate
I can negotiate
I choose to be calm
I choose to be strong
I can live in harmony

I Have Amazing
    & Stunning Bright Eyes!

I Have Gorgeous Skin

It is Beautifully Unique to Me!

Focus on the beauty that is around you. Take deep conscious breaths. Breathe in the joy you feel from focusing on something you love. Feel the energy this brings you, as you slowly breathe out. Imagine your whole body surrounded by this love.

My energy is high.
I stay connected with the
beauty of something I love.
Seeing the color of this
love swirling around my
body, energizes my soul.
I breathe it in and out.

I AM SO READY
FOR MY DAY!

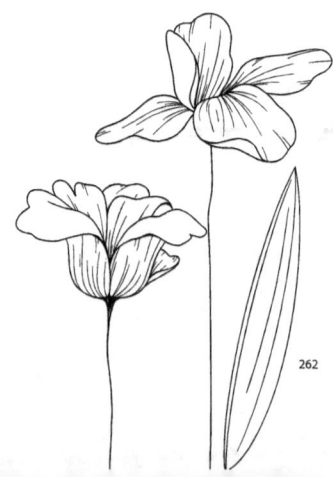

> Can you take a look at a map of the world or imagine it in your head? I want you to mark on that map a little red dot to indicate you. Then I want you to mark more little red dots on that world map that make up your family and friends. Then I want you to imagine how many other little red dots there are across the whole entire world. One little red dot for each person. When you do this, does it really matter what one person says about you? Or even what ten people say about you? They are just a few little red dots in a sea of billions of dots across the whole entire world.
>
> You are special! There are billions of people out there that would think so too if they met you.

I AM

an Important
Part of this World

I learn from my
past mistakes.

I don't need to repeat them.
(and I don't)

I do not try to control other
people's destiny, just as
I don't allow other people
to control mine.

I give out the same positive energy that I wish to receive in return.

> I spread joy across the world,
> by being kind to those around me.

I stay open. There is no need for me to get defensive. Arguing or trying to convince someone of who I am is a waste of energy that I can use to enjoy living my life. Living my truth, speaking my truth... that's how people see the real me; by living as me.

I release anger and fear.
They stem from a feeling
of somehow I am worth less.
I let it go with love. I know
that I'm worthy of all that is
positive, wonderful & great.

> There are no negative events.
>
> Our emotions attached to the event, determine whether it is good or bad. We can actually choose to let the emotion go. Perhaps it's not the right time for the new relationship or perhaps there is a better job just around the corner. Sometimes we have held onto something for far too long, which then causes us great pain when we finally let it go.
>
> By letting go and allowing life to flow, for us to show up and live, we can welcome new experiences in and out of our lives, as simply passing moments. When we cling, we feel pain. When we let go, we feel free.
>
> Let Go.
>
> It's time. You don't need to hold on to any old ideas, names, hurts. It's OK to let go. There is more to you than your past story and everyone around you is lucky to see it unfold; to see you flourish.

66

I am free of my past and it feels amazing!

I trust life to be wonderful.

I am extraordinary!

I am loved & supported by All those around me.

New doors open for me today YAY!
I have every reason to be excited!

> I Am Good Enough...
>
> See how truly
> Amazing you are.

I trust in my abilities...

I am talented in different ways to others.

Every thought in my head I choose. I choose what I think about and how I feel. I am free to choose... so today I pick the ones that make me feel good.

You already know the answer.

Ask for guidance from inside you and listen to your feelings; the instincts within.

Pick one thing right now and say thank you for it. If you can physically <u>see</u> the thing that you are grateful for, then that is already a gift. Good ol' eyesight! It's wonderful to see colors and read this book, take in a child's smile or watch the twinkle in your loved one's eyes.

"Thank you for my perfect eyes"

What else are you thankful for?

You are exactly where
you are meant to be
right at this moment.
It will all work out.
It's up to you to change
what you want to change.
No one else can do that for you,
but there is plenty of help
around if you need it.
Just ask.

*This moment can change,
as can all moments. I can ask
for help when I need it.*

I can do anything and everything.
I hold the remote control to my life.

Just be YOU.

You are the best possible you,
you can be.

REMEMBER

You are Truly Amazing

Do you think your creator wants you to stay in a state of pain and sadness? Whoever you believe in, God, Allah, Buddha, Lord Krishna, the Universe… you were created to live; to live with Joy, to live with Love. No great creator would want you to feel constant pain and suffering. You are a beautiful human being.

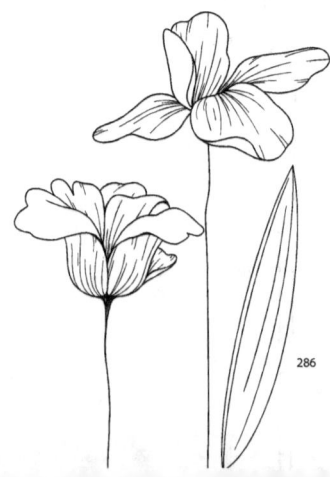

I am the only person that sabotages me... So guess what! I now make choices that bring me joy and give me the best possible chance for a life I love!

I ♡ My Body

I ♡ My Mind

I ♡ My Heart

I ♡ Being a Woman

I ♡ Being Me

There are 3 steps to
accomplish great things:

Plan, Act, Believe.

I know you can do it.
I believe in you. It's time
you believed in you too.

I overflow with
Love & Energy.

And it feels really good!

I love to smile
I love to laugh

And I AM HAPPY.

> I AM Beautiful and Healthy.
>
> I'm lucky to have what I have.
> I appreciate my body.

I have a perfect body!

I fill my body with goodness.
I take good care of me.

When you don't complete a goal or a task, or you avoid having that difficult conversation because you are too busy at work, you're cleaning up, making a phone call, too tired, someone else needs me...
I call BULLSHIT!

We can busy ourselves and hide behind excuses to avoid all that we know needs to be done. But once it's done, it's no longer in your head. It frees up time, space and energy, for all the things you love.

No wastage of time. Continue until the goal is accomplished.

and Remember...
You are Good Enough!

Say it 3 times

"I Am Good Enough"
"I Am Good Enough"
"I Am Good Enough"

> Today I choose to do
> what I have been avoiding.

I am intelligent enough.
I got this... I believe in me.

*This is from 365: Positive Words for a Teenage Girl -I had to include it, cause it works.

You know how this works now -so it's your turn! It's time to put pen to paper and write your own affirmation. You can write one, two or even three if you like -the important thing is that you write at least one. Pick something you like about yourself and write it on a piece of paper and stick it somewhere where you will see it every day. That could be a spot next to your bed or on a mirror, in a diary or even in your wallet. Read this note every single day.

*I know this stuff sounds silly, but if it makes you feel good, that's all that matters. Give it a go... see if it works.

*This is from 365: Positive Words for a Teenage Girl -I had to include this one too.

Now for something a little different but equally as important. Pick something you don't like about yourself and turn it into a positive. For instance, I don't like my hair and I don't like it when I get angry. So I wrote on a piece of paper, "I have beautiful shinny healthy hair" and "I remain calm in every situation and I listen to what others have to say." Now it's your turn. You can write one, two or ten of them if you want to. Read them every day and watch how magically your thoughts and actions can change.

My Destiny is...

Write the life that you want here — no rules — you can have all that you desire...

_____

_____

_____

_____

_____

_____

Close your eyes and see what you desire. Really feel how good it feels.

You can have this. It's time to make the plan and put the plan into Action.

You got this.

I create what I want...

and what I want is...

_____

_____

_____

_____

_____

I am clear on what I want and
I welcome it into my life...
I know I can have it!
I deserve it! And I am
so thankful for it!

I dedicate time everyday,
visualizing my goals,
seeing a clear path to
achieving them and
taking action from my plan
to see them come to fruition.
Life is Good!

I go beyond any limitation.

I believe in me.

I can do it.

I AM LIMITLESS

All my desires I see.
I can bring them into my life.

I can create the life I want.

IMAGINE, ACTION, MANIFEST

Just like running a marathon, it's each individual step you take that gets you to the finish line. It may be really hard and you may want to stop, to give up, but if you keep putting one foot in front of the other, you can get there. It'll never be this hard again. Once you've done it, you've done it. And if you choose to do it again, you can do it with more ease, with the knowledge of how it's done.

I GOT THIS!

Bring on Today!

I allow my creativity to flow
without inhibition nor question.
I pray that loving people surround
and support me and that
I always have the tools
to follow through and complete
the task with love in my heart.

With Planning, Action & Belief, you really can achieve anything you want. Start with a plan today.

Goal:

Steps to get there:

Immediate action to take:

Week 1 action to take:

Week 2 action to take:

Week 3 action to take:

✳✳✳

Look at your goal daily and visualize yourself attaining your goal. See and feel what that looks like. Feel yourself accomplishing it. When you see it, you believe it and when you believe it, you get it done.

✳✳✳

Success comes to me now!

Now really smile.
Feel as though all the success
you want is really here
right now.

Feel it & Repeat:

Success is Here and Now
in My Life!

What do you really want?

What will you do with it once you have received it?

Purpose for what you want, will give you the drive to get you what you want.

Purpose = Passion
Passion = Drive
Drive = Action

I appreciate what I have in my life and the people who love me. I can show my appreciation with the words Thank You.

I compliment others and let them
know how much they mean to me.
When others feel good,
I feel good too.

Now is the time for fruition.
All my dreams now come to pass.
It's worth my time and energy to
complete the necessary work
to achieve my goals.

I can release and let go of any fear or doubt. I trust and know, that with the right plan and action, it can be mine.

Belief, Plan, Action
—with this I can achieve.

Being Beautifully STRONG

"

I can accomplish extraordinary things!

I am a successful and beautiful person.

I Am <u>Extremely</u>:

Beautiful
Intelligent
Imaginative
Creative
Decisive

And anything else I choose to be!

Being Beautifully STRONG

I Am <u>Extremely</u>:

_____

_____

_____

What else would you like to be?

Write down some of the greatest accolades or nicest comments you have received.

_____

_____

_____

_____

Believe the nice things that people say to you. Acknowledge it with, "thank you."

People tell you how wonderful you are, because you are wonderful. The more you say thank you, instead of deflecting, the more you will feel it too.

Today I really believe that
I am wonderful.

My skin is exquisite and
it is unique to me.

I'm allowed to love me
just as I am.

Perfection comes from
imperfections.

I can hold my head high,
knowing I am my perfect me.

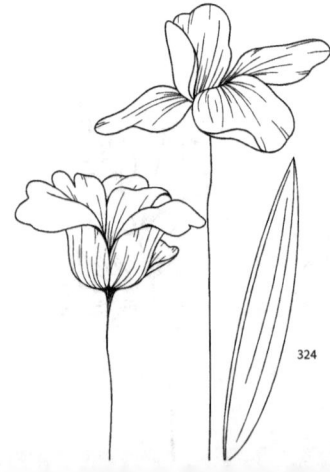

I Respect and Like who I AM.

I am worth the time and effort to take care of me.

I can let go of those who would harm me.

It is safe for me to make choices that inspire me and give me a better life.

"

I create peace & harmony. I always act from personal power. Love surrounds and protects me. I am enthusiastic. I am balanced. I am receiving my amazing continuously. It's never ending, the good in my life. I let life flow.

I have a wonderful life
full of love and laughter.
I am surrounded by amazing
people who love me and I love them.
I am an amazing beautiful
person with stunning bright eyes
and a gorgeous smile.
I am beautiful, kind & caring.

Spend time with those you love. Sometimes we get caught up and annoyed at silly things. Will they really matter once we are gone? Time is short, but it's also long... choose who you spend it with wisely.

Those who drain you, who suck you dry, call you names and put you down... spending time with them is a waste of your life. Love feels good. Friendship feels good. If it doesn't feel good, then ask yourself why you spend time with those people at all?

"

I release the fear of being alone, for I am never truly alone. It is safe for me to let people go.

I choose people in my life that are kind and supportive, just like I am to those who are around me.

If this week was your last week on this earth, what would you do?

What's stopping you from doing it now? When you are gone from this earth, do you think it will really matter if you wore the right shoes, had the right color hair, how long your nails were? I'm guessing other people's opinions won't matter all that much, so how about you start living for you. Stop listening to the negative things people say to you. Start trusting in your own heart and don't be afraid to take a chance on that dream job or telling that special someone how you really feel.

Have Fun. Live full, live in joy and spread that joy to all those who cross your path.

Be Here.

Always living out there, next week, next month, next year, when I meet the guy, buy the car, buy the house, have the kid...

Be Here.

This moment will pass and it will never be lived again. Find the beauty in this moment; a smile, a cup of tea, good coffee, a peaceful nights sleep. Whatever it may be, feel the joy in being right here, right now, in this very moment... then let that one go too.

Be Here.

> I listen to other people, their say and how they feel. I can stay present in this moment without thinking of what next I'm going to say.

I can trust my instincts to tell
me when something isn't right.
I know the feeling,
I can choose to listen
and act accordingly to it.

I choose today to give myself the best life ever! All my wishes and dreams are here and now.

I am grateful.

Thank you for me, for this world -for all that I have.

Thank you for

………………..

This person has helped me so much in my life. I am truly grateful for them.

Know you can...

Now do it!

Being Beautifully STRONG

Perseverance
Preparation
Plan

Then take action...
one step at a time.

Pick Yourself Up and Just Do It!

> You need to be 100% for you as well as for others. Look after yourself.

I AM

Healthy, Rested, Energized.

I am a priority. I take good care of me.

Miracles occur in My Life.

Today I choose to Live in Joy.

> If I choose to be unhappy, it's my choice. If I choose to live in abuse, that is also my choice. Perhaps I don't see that I am worth unconditional love, respect, care, a positive happy life, without conflict. If I remain in conflict, that is my choice.
>
> Can anyone really change this for me? It is my choice to stay in a situation, as it is my choice to move out of a situation.
>
> I must also respect the choices others make. I am here for those who ask for my help, but I must respect their decisions.
>
> We are all worth so much more than we see. Today I choose to see what a beautiful person I am; what beautiful people we can all be.
>
> If you fear for the safety of someone living in abuse, please contact the police and seek professional help.

I am a calm, confident, centered, powerful, strong woman. I receive all that I ask for. I am the luckiest girl in the world. Love, success, fortune, are abundant in my life.
I am incredibly talented.
I am excited and full of life.
The more love and energy I give, the more love and energy I have to give. I am passionate, loving, caring and kind.
I am compassionate. I am sexy, I am stunning, I am incredibly intelligent. I am amazing.
And I am worth it.

I am extraordinary. I have a gorgeous face and body. I have beautiful hair and vibrant youthful skin. I live an amazing fantastic fun life, which I love and I am very grateful for. I love every day.
I love every moment.
I love this moment. Thank you!
I love all people exactly as they are. I am always smiling.
People feel loved by me and comfortable around me. I bring people love and laughter.
I am charismatic!

Nothing is impossible. I am motivated. I am inspired. I am full of joy and I bring joy to others. I have great love in my life. I am greatly loved. I am surrounded by people who love and care about me and want the best for me. I am a strong and worthy woman.

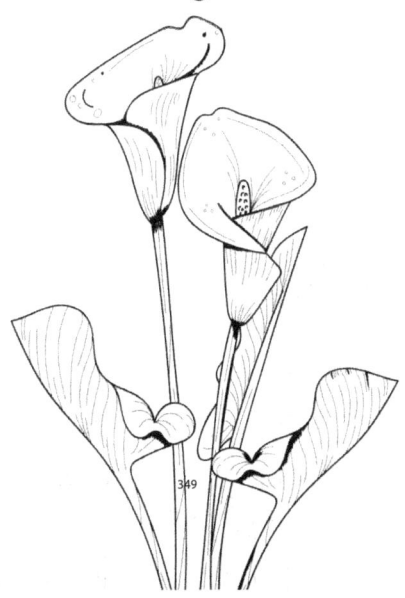

I am excited about life!
My life can change at any
second of any day.

Got a big job, career or dream and your family or friends aren't supportive…

"I could cry about just how unsupportive they are, OR I can just get on with the job and support myself."

❝

-My RSVP for the rest of the year....

"I'm Busy."

If you have a massive dream, an important goal, it's up to you to decide where your time is better spent -in endeavors that make you happy rather than with people who make you feel less?

You are influenced by those who surround you.

Choose wisely.

Persist
Pursue
Endure

-no one can believe for you-

Don't be afraid to work hard for what you want. It is your choice. If you want something for your life, you can choose to work hard for it.

Work is my choice!
I choose it wisely.

Don't be afraid to believe in Miracles.

They happen.

I am not going to begin explaining particles, subatomic particles, atoms nor nuclei (I'm clearly no scientist but I read). What is suggested, is that we are all made up of energy. Everything is. When you get down to the very core, everything is energy. So if particles move and vibrate to form matter, and the particles at the very core are made up of energy, then we can change energy, which we do with our thoughts and feelings, and feelings are determined by our thoughts. So basically we really are only limited by our thinking!

That was my fun fact ☺ but don't take my word for it, read about it yourself.

Always remember what I said earlier; don't take anything you read or hear as gospel truth, investigate for yourself. That's the only way you'll know for sure!

***

We learn and grow. Don't ever be embarrassed about the shit you have been through. Share it with others so that they may learn without having to suffer through it as you did.

Let's take care of each other.
We all can. So let's choose to.

***

What changes the world is how people feel and you can directly impact how people feel.

When you Act from Love
You Emanate Love.

When People Feel Love
They Give Love.

I know it's not as easy as just doing affirmations to feel good. I want your pain to ease, I want you to see how truly amazing you are and how limitless you are. Don't lose the next ten years doubting yourself nor allowing less in your life or letting someone treat you less than the love you deserve. You (just like everyone else) deserve to live with absolute joy.

I CHOOSE ME
I CHOOSE JOY
I CHOOSE THOSE WHO
SUPPORT ME
LOVE ME
ACCEPT ME
JUST AS I AM

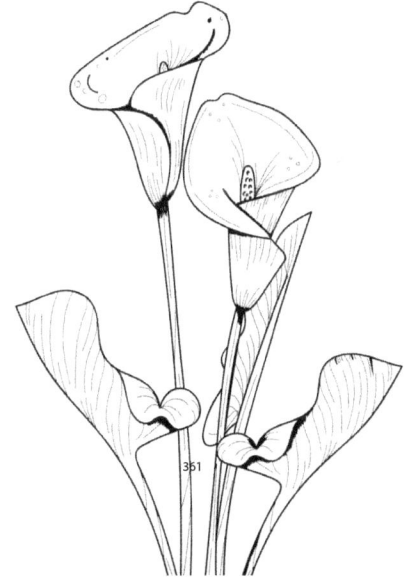

Promise yourself right now that you are always going to love you first. It's time to trust that when you truly love you, so does everybody else.

Always be the kindess person in the room.

Thank You for all the
hard times and lessons
(aka all the shit!)

Look at what I did with it ☺

Being Beautifully STRONG

This was the diary from Venice
that I wrote all of what BB contains.

Turn pain into gratitude. Shift your
attention to what you love and
you will feel better for it.

Thank Yourself!

You did it!

You made the changes!

You believed!

You did the work!

See... I told you, you are amazing!

I AM AMAZING

www.ingramcontent.com/pod-product-compliance
Lightning Source LLC
Chambersburg PA
CBHW071149300426
44113CB00009B/1141